How do I feel about

LONELINESS

AND

MAKING

FRIENDS

Frankl · Sydney

An Aladdin Book
© Aladdin Books Ltd 1996

Designed and produced by
Aladdin Books Ltd
28 Percy Street
London W1P OLD

First published in Great Britain
in 1996 by Franklin Watts
96 Leonard Street
London EC2A 4RH

ISBN: 0 7496 2492 2 (hb)
ISBN : 0 7496 3627 0 (pb)

A catalogue record for this
book is available from the
British Library.

Printed in Belgium

Designer   Tessa Barwick
Editor   Jen Green
Illustrator   Christopher
                O'Neill
Photographer   Roger Vlitos

The author, Sarah Levete,
has edited and written many
books for young people and
children on social issues and
other subjects.

Contents

Introduction

Kev, Amy, Josh and Elly are friends. Friends trust each other and have fun together. Sometimes it's nice to be on your own. At other times if you are alone but want to be with others, you may feel lonely. The four friends will share their ideas on making friends and the ups and downs of friendships.

Sometimes I like being on my own.

I find it hard to make friends.

AMY

JOSH

Friends are great, except when you fall out.

I have a few really close friends.

ELLY

KEV

INVITE

Feeling Lonely

Amy and Kev got chatting when their class went swimming. Amy has just moved to the area. She is telling Kev that she sometimes feels lonely because she doesn't know many people. There are lots of reasons why a person may feel lonely. Have you ever felt lonely?

It can be great to be alone...

...but it can also feel lonely.

▶ It's OK To Be Alone

Being alone does not mean you are lonely. It can be fun to watch a TV programme or read a book all on your own.

At other times, if you want to chat to a friend and there is nobody there, then you may feel lonely.

▼ Do They Like Me?

Sometimes it can seem as if everyone except for you has lots of friends. That can make you feel lonely, and a bit jealous too. Feeling lonely can make you nervous about making new friends.

◀ The Same But Different!

From our heads to our toes, we are all different. But whether you are big or small, or your skin is black or white, we are all people who deserve friendship and respect. It can feel lonely if someone is unkind, or leaves you out because you are different from them. People who do this miss out on good friendships.

5

1. Chaz's dad gave him a game for his birthday. But he had no one to play with.

2. Chaz hoped his new game would help him to make friends at school.

3. Chaz shouted at his dad because the game hadn't made Chaz any friends.

Why was Chaz cross with his dad?

Chaz felt lonely and fed up. He took his feelings out on his dad. That wasn't very fair. It wasn't his dad's fault that Chaz found it difficult to make friends.

Feeling lonely can make you cross and angry with the people who care about you.

It would have made Chaz feel better if he had told his dad how he felt.

▼ I Don't Care . . .

Sometimes feeling lonely can make you feel nasty. You may think that there is no point in being nice to others because you don't have any friends anyway. But being mean will only make you feel more lonely and unhappy.

Why don't you want to go to school?

◀ I'm Scared

Feeling lonely can make you feel less confident. You may not want to go to school because being with lots of other people can make you feel even more alone.

If someone is friendly, you may feel too shy to be friendly back.

This will teach them not to ignore me.

Amy, how did it feel when you were lonely?

"I felt as if nobody would ever like me. I thought I would never have anyone to play with.

When we moved here, I missed my old friends. Everybody at my new school already knew each other, and they all seemed to have friends. I felt cross with my mum for making us move here. But after a while, I began to feel more at home and then I made friends with Elly."

Why Friends Are Important

Josh and Elly are talking about why friends are important to them. Josh enjoys having lots of friends because he can do different things with them. Elly likes being able to tell her friends jokes, even if they don't laugh at them!

Why are friends important to you?

I like rollerblading with some friends and swapping books with others.

I can tell friends things that I can't tell other people.

Friends can trust each other.

8

Friends make some things easier!

▼ Good Times

Have you ever been told a really funny joke and wanted to tell someone else, to make them laugh?

You can share good times with friends. You can have a laugh, even if they tell rotten jokes!

Don't worry. I'll help you.

I'll never be able to do this.

◀ Bad Times

If you've had a difficult day at school or had cross words with your mum or dad, it can really help to talk things over with a friend.

A friend can't make a bad day go away, but it certainly helps to talk.

I've been dying to tell you this all day!

Elly, what do friends mean to you?

"I have a few good friends who matter to me a lot. We can be honest with each other about how we feel. You can talk to friends when you're cross and know that they will understand. Friends are people you trust and who make you feel safe and happy. Mum and dad are my friends too."

Making Friends

Elly and Amy are now good friends, though it took Amy a long time to believe anyone would like her. There are lots of different ways to make friends but it's important to remember that friends are people you can trust. People who make you feel uncomfortable are not friends. If you feel unsure about someone, tell a grown-up.

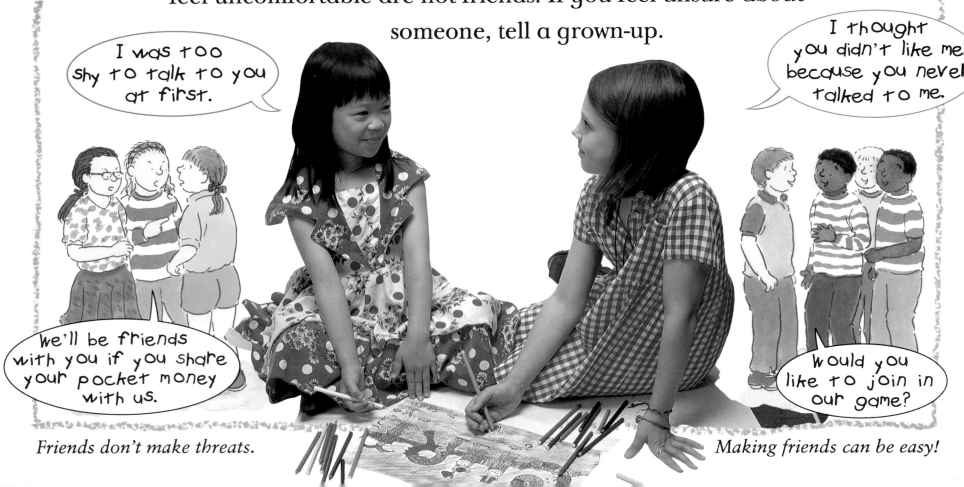

Friends don't make threats.

Making friends can be easy!

▶ *Who Will Notice Me?*

Sometimes it seems as if everyone else is always saying something funny or clever, or has better games to play than you.

Don't worry. Everyone feels like that sometimes. In fact, everyone else is probably feeling the same as you!

▼ *Sing And Dance!*

Have you ever thought of joining a club or a group? It's a great way to meet people. You may feel shy at first, but others probably feel the same.

Making friends can be fun – so why not make a song and dance about it?

◀ *Silent Friends*

A cat or dog can be your friend. So can an imaginary friend that no one else can see.

But it's also important to have "real" friends of your own age, who you can chat to and do things with. Real friends can also cheer you up if you feel sad.

1. Jo wanted to make friends. She tried pushing in, but the others ignored her.

2. Jo gave her sweets away to try and make friends. It didn't work.

3. Jo asked Susie to play. Susie said yes. Jo and Susie became friends.

Jo found it hard to make friends.

There is no magic recipe for making friends. Sometimes it can be easy, but at other times it can feel like very hard work.

As Jo discovered, pushing in doesn't work – it's not very friendly. "Buying" friends doesn't work, either. What happens when you run out of sweets? The best way to make friends is to be friendly, and to be yourself!

▼ Does It Feel OK?

Nobody should offer you presents to make friends with you. People who make threats aren't really friends, either. If a person threatens you or makes you feel uneasy, or says your friendship must be a secret, tell a grown-up you trust.

Would you like to play?

◀ Help Make It Easy

If you see someone who looks a bit lost and alone, why not ask him or her to join in with your friends? It may not make much difference to you, but it may make someone else feel really happy.

Let's be friends. I'll buy you those sweets.

Amy, do you make friends easily?

"Not really. Sometimes I think that nobody will like me – that makes me feel shy. Even though I don't always feel like it, I make an extra effort to be friendly at school. It makes it easier when other people make an effort to include me too. Jan asked me to play and now we're friends.

But I wouldn't be friends if someone offered me presents or made threats. I'd tell my mum."

Different Friendships

Elly is reading Josh a really funny bit from a letter from her friend Ben who lives far away. Elly doesn't see Ben very often but they write to each other. There are lots of different kinds of friendships, from best friends to gangs of friends. Can you think of any other kinds of friendships?

Groups of friends are fun.

Try writing to a friend.

▼ Friends Feel Good!

You may be surprised to realise that your mum, dad, carer, brother or sister is actually good fun as a friend, too.

There are no rules about who you can be friends with, as long as they make you feel good and comfortable.

◀ Best Friends

Some people have several friends, but one *best* friend. This is often the person they feel closest to.

It's great having a best friend, but don't worry if you don't have one. All kinds of friends are equally important.

Josh, tell us about your friends.

"I have lots of different friends. My sister is a good friend, even though I get cross with her when she beats me at football.

My best friend is Toby. We tell each other everything – but I'm not telling you what we say!

Sometimes I go round in a gang and do things with lots of friends – that's fun, too."

15

Difficult Times

Josh is telling Kev that he is cross with his best friend, Toby, because Toby went off and played with someone else. Sometimes even best friends like Josh and Toby have arguments. Being friends with someone isn't always easy. Can you think of reasons why being friends can be difficult?

Friendships can be hard.

Arguments don't last for ever.

◀ Feeling Jealous

You may feel jealous of a friend because he or she has something you want, or has been invited to a party instead of you.

But part of being a friend is enjoying someone else's good luck, however difficult that is!

▶ Don't Worry!

If you have been left out of a game or not invited to someone's party, you will know that it can make you feel fed up and lonely.

Remember, it happens to everyone. It doesn't mean that no one likes you or you will never be included.

▲ What's Gone Wrong?

It is upsetting when a person you like or feel close to, suddenly doesn't want to be your friend. You may not understand why. But friendships do change over time, and we all have to accept that, although it's hard.

1. Penny and Ashika were best friends. They walked to school together.

Hi, Anne. Why don't you walk with us to school?

Hi, Penny.

2. They met another friend of Penny's called Anne. Ashika looked cross.

Why was Ashika cross?

Ashika didn't think that Penny could be friends with Anne as well as her. But Ashika might have liked Anne if she had given her more of a chance.

Sometimes you may feel jealous of the other people your friend likes. But just because a person has more than one friend, it doesn't mean that they like you any less, or that you are less special to them.

No you can't. Penny's my friend.

3. Ashika didn't want Penny to have other friends.

▼ Say NO!

If a friend dares you to do something which you feel is wrong, don't do it, even if he or she makes fun of you. So-called friends like that aren't worth it. It's better to lose a friend, than do something you know is wrong.

> How would you feel if someone did that to you?

◄ Speak Up

No one has the right to hurt someone else or make anyone feel unhappy.

If you see a friend being unkind to someone, explain why you feel what they did was wrong. Friends can be wrong sometimes!

> Dare you to take that comic.

Kev, have you had problems with friends?

"I went round with a gang who started stealing. They told me to keep it a secret, but I didn't want to join in. I talked to my dad and decided to leave the gang. I'm glad I did.

Secrets are great, but there are some secrets which friends shouldn't ask you to keep. If it feels wrong, say 'NO'."

19

Working At Friendships

Kev and Elly are at Josh's birthday party. Josh and his friend
Toby have made up – they are best friends again! Kev and
Elly know that friends can have good and bad times. Being
honest about how you feel can save a friendship. Can you
think of other ways to work at friendships?

If I get cross with a friend it helps if we talk about it.

Friends have to let you be on your own sometimes.

No thanks. I want to read my book!

She's great isn't she?

▼ Try Talking!

If you and a friend have an argument or get cross, talk to each other about how you feel. If you still feel cross with each other, you might ask your mum or dad to sit with you both so you can sort it out.

◄ Make Space!

It's important to think about other people's feelings. Sometimes you may be the centre of attention, and at other times you won't. But remember, there's lots of time for everyone.

I think I understand.

Elly, what are your tips for staying good friends?

"I think that it is important to tell a friend what you are thinking – even if you are really fed up with the person.

Unless you can say sorry and forgive each other, you might stay cross forever. Friends are special – try not to lose them!"

21

Don't Forget . . .

Josh, what do friends mean to you?

"A friend is someone you can be yourself with, even if you are sad or cross. You can have a laugh with a friend. But sometimes you have to say you're sorry, like I did with Toby. Because he's my friend, he didn't stay cross with me – we even joked about it, later."

Elly, is there a difference between being alone and feeling lonely?

"Yes. When you are on your own and feel good about it, that's not feeling lonely. Feeling lonely is when you want to be with a friend, but there is nobody there.

I felt lonely when my friend Ben moved away – I really missed talking to him. I found it hard to make new friends."

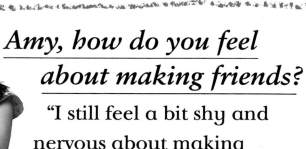

Amy, how do you feel about making friends?

"I still feel a bit shy and nervous about making friends, but I try to make an effort to be friendly.

Elly persuaded me to try for a part in the school play – I met some really nice people there. I think we were all nervous, but once we got talking it was fun. I got a part, too!"

Kev, can you make sure no one feels lonely?

"Not really, but you can try to make everyone feel welcome, especially if they are new to a group. Not everyone finds it easy to make friends. Even if you don't want to be best friends with someone, there's no harm in being nice to them."

Index

All the photographs in this book have been posed by models. The publishers would like to thank them all.